The California Gold Rush: The History and Legacy of the Forty-Niners and America's Golden Dream

By Charles River Editors

Advertisement for sailing to San Francisco amidst the Gold Rush

About Charles River Editors

Charles River Editors was founded by Harvard and MIT alumni to provide superior editing and original writing services, with the expertise to create digital content for publishers across a vast range of subject matter. In addition to providing original digital content for third party publishers, Charles River Editors republishes civilization's greatest literary works, bringing them to a new generation via ebooks.

Introduction

Illustration in Harpers Ferry of a "49er" panning gold

The Gold Rush

"As the spring and summer of 1848 advanced, the reports came faster and faster from the gold-mines at Sutter's saw-mill. Stories reached us of fabulous discoveries, and spread throughout the land. Everybody was talking of "Gold! gold!!" until it assumed the character of a fever. Some of our soldiers began to desert; citizens were fitting out trains of wagons and pack-mules to go to the mines. We heard of men earning fifty, five hundred, and thousands of dollars per day..." – William Tecumseh Sherman

One of the most important and memorable events of the United States' westward push across the frontier came with the discovery of gold in the lands that became California in January 1848. Located thousands of miles away from the country's power centers on the east coast at the time, the announcement came a month before the Mexican-American War had ended, and among the very few Americans that were near the region at the time, many of them were Army soldiers who were participating in the war and garrisoned there. San Francisco was still best known for being a Spanish military and missionary outpost during the colonial era, and only a few hundred called it home. Mexico's independence, and its possession of those lands, had come only a generation earlier.

Everything changed almost literally overnight. While the Mexican-American War technically concluded with a treaty in February 1948, the announcement brought an influx of an estimated 90,000 "Forty-Niners" to the region in 1849, hailing from other parts of America and even as far away as Asia. All told, an estimated 300,000 people would come to California over the next few years, as men dangerously trekked thousands of miles in hopes of making a fortune, and in a span of months, San Francisco's population exploded, making it one of the first mining boomtowns to truly spring up in the West. This was a pattern that would repeat itself across the West anytime a mineral discovery was made, from the Southwest and Tombstone to the Dakotas and Deadwood. Of course, that was made possible by the collective memory of the original California gold rush.

Despite the mythology and the romantic portrayals that helped make the California Gold Rush, most of the individuals who came to make a fortune struck out instead. The gold rush was a boon to business interests, which ensured important infrastructure developments like the railroad and the construction of westward paths, but ultimately, it also meant that big business reaped most of the profits associated with mining the gold. While the Forty-Niners are often remembered for panning gold out of mountain streams, it required advanced mining technology for most to make a fortune.

Nevertheless, the California Gold Rush became an emblem of the American Dream, and the notion that Americans could obtain untold fortunes regardless of their previous social status. As historian H.W. Brands said of the impact the gold rush had on Americans at the time, "The old American Dream ... was the dream of the Puritans, of Benjamin Franklin's 'Poor Richard'... of men and women content to accumulate their modest fortunes a little at a time, year by year by year. The new dream was the dream of instant wealth, won in a twinkling by audacity and good luck... [it] became a prominent part of the American psyche only after Sutter's Mill." While the gold rush may not have every Forty-Niner rich, the events still continue to influence the country's collective mentality.

This book comprehensively covers the history and legacy of the gold rush that took place from 1848-1855, analyzing how it affected the participants and the nation at large. Along with pictures and a bibliography, you will learn about the California Gold Rush like you never have before, in no time at all.

Chapter 1: The Source of California's Gold

400 million years ago, California existed as a chain of offshore islands and a seafloor dominated by underwater hot springs. While the ash and lavas slowly built up the land area of California itself, the deposits of sulfides proved the most important resource for California's future: gold. The next 200 million years witnessed a period of titanic crustal collisions, as the offshore islands were crushed and folded, along with the volcanic rocks. This metamorphic process created a significant layer of bedrock of the gold areas of future California, known as the Mother Lode region, and the end of the 200 million period resulted in the tectonic forces of the planet pushing the Californian sea floor underneath the North American continent.

The materials did not rest in the subduction zone but rose to the surface of the crust, melted into magma by the interior heat of the planet. The materials then came to the surface through the power of volcanic eruptions, and as the lava cooled slowly, it formed the granitic rock of a giant mountain range, the Sierra Nevadas.[1] From there, water and heat served as the main agents of the dispersal of gold into the Sierra Nevadas. Rain and melted snow percolated into the ground and came into contact with hot molten magma, dissolving the mineral resources, which consisted not only of gold but also other precious m metals like quartz, silver, copper, and zinc. A stew was produced of metals and sulfides and rose to the surface through the fractures in the crust. The stew finally dried as quartz veins in the rocks or came to the surface in the process of hydrothermal mineralization.

When the forces of erosion stripped these layers of rock, they exposed the veins of gold to the elements and began to carry gold particles down the sides of mountains. Some gold was deposited in stream beds, other particles were left as patches of gold on the sides of mountains or valley plateaus, and other gold was covered up by lava flows and layers of sediment.[2]

---

[1] Garry Hayes, "Mining History and Geology of the California Gold Rush," http://hayesg.faculty.mjc.edu/Gold_Rush.html;
[2] Garry Hayes, "Mining History and Geology of the California Gold Rush," http://hayesg.faculty.mjc.edu/Gold_Rush.html;

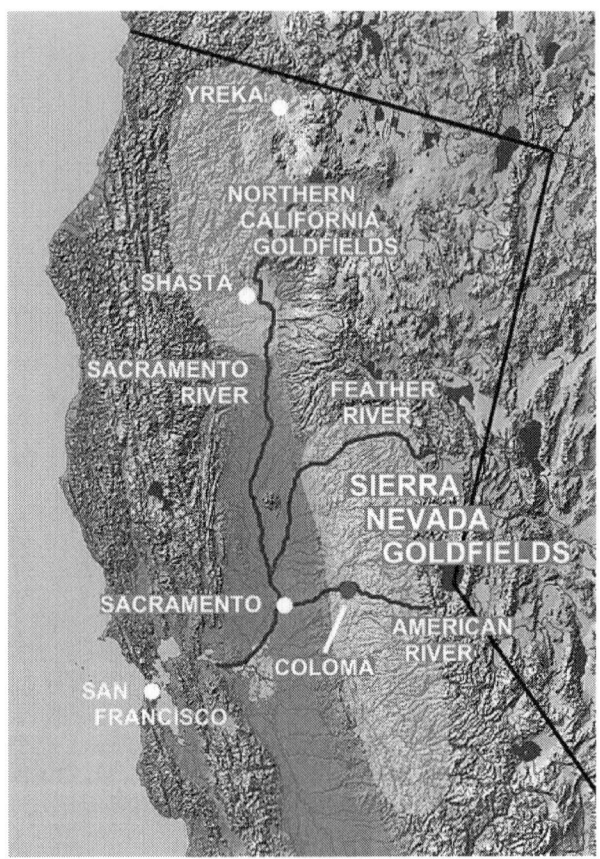

The main goldfields in California

The most important thing was the location of the gold, as most of it lay on the surface of the ground. It belonged to no one except the people who were willing to accomplish the tough work of mining the element.

Chapter 2: The Discovery of Gold

1850 picture of Sutter's Mill

The discovery of California's abundant gold was made in such an inauspicious manner that it was almost too amazing to be believed. While Mexicans from the state of Sonora immigrated to California for the purpose of mining, the American adventurers before 1848 had come for a climate and soil conducive for agriculture. Mexico had long meant to find colonists for the region, and Americans, along with Britons, made acceptable applicants. The new landowners saw plenty of room to dominate the region, given the ease to hold large land grants; and many thought of themselves as "new" Californio land barons.

John Sutter belonged to this generation of rare men that settled California with dreams of amassing a huge plot of land. Sutter was a Mexican citizen who had been born in Germany, and near New Helvetia (present-day Sacramento), he planned to sell lumber for building purposes in the region. On the south fork of the American River, Sutter hired another American, James Marshall, to build and operate a sawmill with him.

Photo of Sutter circa 1850

James W. Marshall

Needing workers, Marshall hired former soldiers from the Mormon Battalion who had stayed on in California after the Mexican-American War. Many were in California for religious reasons; they had been part of Brigham Young's trek to the Great Salt Basin in Utah, and they saw the chance to live in California as an opportunity to open more of the west to the Kingdom of Zion.

Many Mormon soldiers had participated in the opening of the "Mormon Corridor," as southern California was called, and they had prepared to return back to newly-risen Salt Lake City, the capital of the Mormon-controlled State of Deseret. If not for an epistle written especially for the Californian Saints, and the placement and influence of a powerful Mormon in San Francisco, the Mormons never would have been present as laborers at Sutter's sawmill on the American River, the place where surface gold was first discovered.[3]

---

[3] The Discovery of Gold in California (California Geological Survey - Gold Discovery)

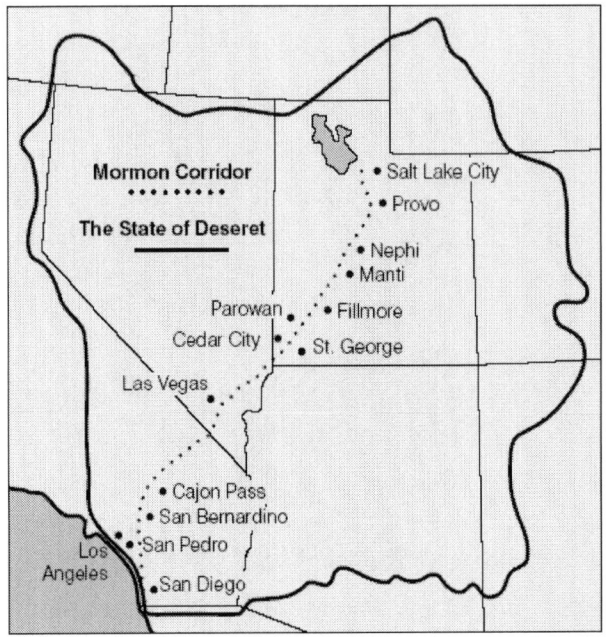

Mormon laborers worked on Sutter's mill to increase the flow of water into the waterwheel. The digging of dirt, blasting of boulders, and moving of granite made the river's fork deeper and wider. The work also upset the composition of the earth. What happened next was recorded in two sources, long after the event. The first was written by James Marshall in 1857, as he related what happened on January 24, 1848.[4]

> "I used to go down in the morning to see what had been done by the water through the night; and about half past seven o'clock on or about the 19th of January—I am not quite certain of a day, but it was between the 18th and 20th of that month—1848, I went down as usual . . . [near] the lower end [of the mill race], . . . upon the rock, about six inches beneath the surface of the water, I DIS-COVERED THE GOLD. I was entirely alone at the time, I picked up one or two pieces and examined them attentively."[5]

---

[4] The Discovery of Gold in California (California Geological Survey - Gold Discovery)
[5] M. Guy Bishop, "A Place in History: The Impact of Sutter's Mill Gold Discovery on Henry Bigler," *Nauvoo Journal*, 103-104, James W. Marshall, as quoted in Hutchings California Magazine (Sacramento,
[5]California) 2 [November 1857]: 201,
[5]http://mormonhistoricsites.org/wp-content/uploads/2013/05/NJ11.1_Bishop.pdf

But the only way the date had been fully established is through the study of the journal of Henry Bigler, one of the Mormon workmen. Bigler had written, "On January 24th while looking at the race, through which a little water was running, [Marshall] saw something yellow on the bedrock. . . . Just before we quit work for the day Marshall came up and told us he believed he had found a gold mine."[6]

Of course, farmers and carpenters were not authorities on the topic of precious metals, so Sutter and Marshall literally did not yet know what they had on their hands. Marshall explained the initial discovery, which came about as he was investigating the channel of the stream nearby:

> "I picked up one or two pieces and examined them attentively; and having some general knowledge of minerals, I could not call to mind more than two which in any way resembled this, sulphuret of iron, very bright and brittle; and gold, bright, yet malleable. I then tried it between two rocks, and found that it could be beaten into a different shape, but not broken. I then collected four or five pieces and went up to Mr. Scott (who was working at the carpenters bench making the mill wheel) with the pieces in my hand and said, 'I have found it.'
>
> 'What is it?' inquired Scott.
>
> 'Gold,' I answered.
>
> 'Oh! no,' replied Scott, 'That can't be.'
>
> I said,--'I know it to be nothing else.'

---

[6] M. Guy Bishop, "A Place in History: The Impact of Sutter's Mill Gold Discovery on Henry Biggler," *Nauvoo Journal*, 105, [Henry W. Bigler] "Diary of H. W. Bigler in 1847 and 1848," John S. Hittell, ed.,
[6] Overland Monthly 10 (September 1887): 242, http://mormonhistoricsites.org/wp-content/uploads/2013/05/NJ11.1_Bishop.pdf

The location of Marshall's discovery

Sure enough, Marshall had found gold just days before the Mexican-American war was ending. Marshall brought up his discovery with Sutter, and the men operating the sawmill performed tests to ensure it was gold. Ironically, Sutter wanted to keep the discovery quiet because he was concerned that it would disrupt his plan to farm in the region and make it that much harder for him to claim title to the nearby lands that he wanted.

Naturally, keeping this kind of secret among several people proved impossible. Other workers on Sutter's Mill also began to find gold, and as more and more people found gold, they didn't exactly want to keep cutting wood. When employees from the mill began to turn up in San Francisco and buy goods with gold, newspaperman Samuel Brannan took notice. As a member of the Mormon Church, Brannan dreamed of a western kingdom for the Saints, and Brannan had lucked out. He lived in a location on the bay that, while not strong in geography, could boast a collection of entrepreneurial merchants who supported the vision of San Francisco as a key port city to command finance and capital for a powerful California. When Brannan learned of the discovery of gold from fellow Mormons in his employ, the city of San Francisco was but a dream; people still called the location "Yerba Buena." Sandbars surrounded parts of the city, estuaries were long and marshy places that refused to port ocean-going ships, and banks of fog and wind swept over a dry, hilly peninsula covered in places by dunes.

Brannan

Eventually, Brannan headed to the mill as a representative for the Latter Day Saints, ostensibly to collect tithes from Mormon workers. But when Brannan also found gold near Sutter's Mill, he intended to do exactly what one would expect a writer to do: write about it. There was just one problem; many of the paper's employees had already set off in search of gold themselves. As one biography of Brannan put it, "Brannan moved to New Helvetia, where he opened a store at John Sutter's Fort. When gold was discovered, Brannan owned the only store between San Francisco and the gold fields -- a fact he capitalized on by buying up all the picks, shovels and pans he could find, and then running up and down the streets of San Francisco, shouting 'Gold! Gold on the American River!'"

Like many opportunists, Brannan would make his fortune not by mining gold but by selling goods to the miners. Brannan used news of the discovery of gold at Sutter's Mill as a form of advertisement that allowed him to dominate the mercantile potential of a young California and use the location to stage an economic empire. He found Yerba Buena as a town of huts and dunes and left it a city of San Francisco with shops and brick streets. Imperial San Francisco was born, and it, along with its merchants who sold materials to the first miners, would ultimately command the Gold Rush.[7]

The myth of Brannan waving a bottle of gold in the streets of San Francisco is less important than the impulse of business men just like him to make San Francisco the economic capital of California and the most important city on the West Coast. Their mercantile ambitions ensured that a powerful state would rise around San Francisco, and the population would increase, as the point of entry for thousands of miners to travel to the gold fields in the Northern and Southern Mines.[8]

The *Californian* did, in fact, advertise on March 15, 1848 about the discovery of gold at Sutter's Mill, but the notice received little attention until Brannan's association of merchants backed the news and made it important enough for the first Californians -- not only Californios and Native Americans, but Mexican-American War veterans -- to operate on a low-technological level. As the California Geological Survey explains, these early miners were initially stooped over, immersed in the freezing rivers, and working from sunup to sundown:

> "The crude method of pen-knife and butcher-knife mining soon gave way to more adequate methods of placer mining. The batea, or dish shaped Indian basket, the iron gold pan, and the cradle, which were used to expedite the process of separation of gold and sediment, were soon in evidence. The cradle (or rocker as it was often called) proved to be inefficient because of the loss of many of the small particles, and was soon improved. The new development was the long tom, an elongated, non-rocking cradle in which transverse cleats arrested these small gold particles. Soon, however, the long tom was superseded by sluices of various types."[9]

---

[7] "Map of San Francisco Showing Business Section and Waterfront, 1851 - 1852," http://www.ronhenggeler.com/History/yerba_buena/1851map.htm; The Virtual Museum of the City of San Francisco, "From the 1820s to the Gold Rush," http://www.sfmuseum.org/hist1/early.html; "The Renaming of San Francisco," http://www.sfmuseum.net/hist/name.html

[8] Gold Rush (Part Four: The Legacy), "Businesses, Banks Cashed in by 'Mining the Miners,'" http://www.calgoldrush.com/lb_sets/04business.html

[9] The Discovery of Gold in California (California Geological Survey - Gold Discovery)

A man panning for gold

Sluicing to separate the gold from the dirt and water

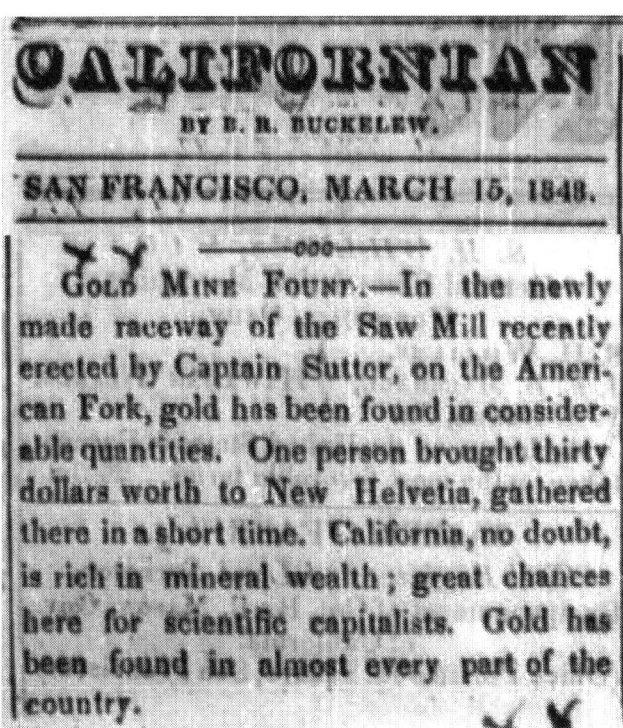

Announcement of the discovery of gold

Army officer William Tecumseh Sherman, who would later become a legend during the Civil War, was stationed near San Francisco when gold was discovered, and he wrote of the initial discovery in his memoirs:

> "I remember one day, in the spring of 1848, that two men, Americans, came into the office and inquired for the Governor. I asked their business, and one answered that they had just come down from Captain Sutter on special business, and they wanted to see Governor Mason in person. I took them in to the colonel, and left them together. After some time the colonel came to his door and called to me. I went in, and my attention was directed to a series of papers unfolded on his table, in which lay about half an ounce of placer-gold. Mason said to me, "What is that?" I touched it and examined one or two of the larger pieces, and asked, "Is it gold?" Mason asked me if I had ever seen native gold. I answered that, in 1844, I was in Upper Georgia, and there saw some native gold, but it was much finer than this, and it was

in phials, or in transparent quills; but I said that, if this were gold, it could be easily tested, first, by its malleability, and next by acids. I took a piece in my teeth, and the metallic lustre was perfect. I then called to the clerk, Baden, to bring an axe and hatchet from the backyard. When these were brought I took the largest piece and beat it out flat, and beyond doubt it was metal, and a pure metal. Still, we attached little importance to the fact, for gold was known to exist at San Fernando, at the south, and yet was not considered of much value.

Colonel Mason then handed me a letter from Captain Sutter, addressed to him, stating that he (Sutter) was engaged in erecting a saw-mill at Coloma, about forty miles up the American Fork, above his fort at New Helvetia, for the general benefit of the settlers in that vicinity; that he had incurred considerable expense, and wanted a 'preëmption' to the quarter-section of land on which the mill was located, embracing the tail-race in which this particular gold had been found. Mason instructed me to prepare a letter, in answer, for his signature. I wrote off a letter, reciting that California was yet a Mexican province, simply held by us as a conquest; that no laws of the United States yet applied to it, much less the land laws or preëmption laws, which could only apply after a public survey. Therefore it was impossible for the Governor to promise him (Sutter) a title to the land; yet, as there were no settlements within forty miles, he was not likely to be disturbed by trespassers. Colonel Mason signed the letter, handed it to one of the gentlemen who had brought the sample of gold, and they departed.

That gold was the first discovered in the Sierra Nevada, which soon revolutionized the whole country, and actually moved the whole civilized world."

Sherman himself eventually saw Sutter's Mill and explained how its operations made it suitable for also mining gold: "Labor was very scarce, expensive, and had to be economized. The mill was built over a dry channel of the river which was calculated to be the tail-race. After arranging his head-race, dam and tub-wheel, he let on the water to test the goodness of his machinery. It worked very well until it was found that the tail-race did not carry off the water fast enough, so he put his men to work in a rude way to clear out the tail-race. They scratched a kind of ditch down the middle of the dry channel, throwing the coarser stones to one side; then, letting on the water again, it would run with velocity down the channel, washing away the dirt, thus saving labor. This course of action was repeated several times, acting exactly like the long Tom afterward resorted to by the miners."

Ironically, the people most responsible for discovering gold were also among the hardest hit by the discovery. Sutter couldn't control the employees on his sawmill once rumors of Marshall's discovery made their way around, as Sherman explained, "Marshall returned to the mill, but could not keep out of his wonderful ditch, and by some means the other men employed there learned his secret. They then wanted to gather the gold, and Marshall threatened to shoot them if they attempted it; but these men had sense enough to know that if "placer"-gold existed at Coloma, it would also be found farther down-stream, and they gradually "prospected" until they reached Mormon Island, fifteen miles below, where they discovered one of the richest placers on earth. These men revealed the fact to some other Mormons who were employed by Captain Sutter at a grist-mill he was building still lower down the American Fork, and six miles above his fort. All of them struck for high wages, to which Sutter yielded, until they asked ten dollars a day, which he refused, and the two mills on which he had spent so much money were never built, and fell into decay." In addition to Sutter's Mill never flourishing, Marshall himself would die penniless, not getting in on the gold rush early enough and then losing money when he did enter the business years down the line.

If anything, the ability to mine surface gold -- placer mining -- required a society to be built up from scratch at it most rudimentary level. While 1849 is often remembered as the year of the Gold Rush, the miners that came the year after the discovery greatly relied upon the people who were already there. The local society boosted the opportunity of gold mining from the beginning, and it required people already in the vicinity to create and maintain the first towns in the Sierra Nevada foothills. The '48ers, as history has called them, created the infrastructure that would support the Gold Rush, which would lure about 300,000 miners when it was all said and done. people at-work in the end. Dale Kassler wrote, "The discovery of gold spawned the stunningly swift development of a sophisticated market-driven economy run by bankers, venture capitalists, importers, experts and merchants of all kind, including many who once had tried their hands at mining. It was an economy that made tycoons out of people like Levi Strauss, a dry-goods merchant from Bavaria, and the slick real estate speculators who bought and sold parcels of land in Sacramento on an almost daily basis. There were corporations established to move people and provisions from San Francisco to Sacramento. There were companies that bought gold dust and companies that minted coins and companies that did both."

While the people near San Francisco quickly began rushing toward the area where gold was discovered, it still took a lot of time for news to travel, and the discovery of gold did not truly lead to a "rush" until the announcement from President James Polk near the end of the year. Victory in the Mexican-American War (1846-1848) had given America a "golden California," and by the end of the year, as if guided by divine providence, the state seemed prepared to live up to its promise. Polk announced to Congress that December:

> "It was known that mines of the precious metals existed to a considerable extent in California at the time of its acquisition. Recent discoveries render it probable that these mines are more extensive and valuable than was anticipated. The accounts of the abundance of gold in that territory are of such an extraordinary character as would scarcely command belief were they not corroborated by the authentic reports of officers in the public service who have visited the mineral district and derived the facts which they detail from personal observation. Reluctant to credit the reports in general circulation as to the quantity of gold, the officer commanding our forces in

California visited the mineral district in July last for the purpose of obtaining accurate information on the subject. His report to the War Department of the result of his examination and the facts obtained on the spot is herewith laid before Congress. When he visited the country there were about 4,000 persons engaged in collecting gold. There is every reason to believe that the number of persons so employed has since been augmented. The explorations already made warrant the belief that the supply is very large and that gold is found at various places in an extensive district of country."[10]

Perhaps the delivery of wealth eased Polk's mind about the decision to forcibly annex California, and the manner in which he led the nation into the Mexican-American War as a whole, but the problems of gold almost immediately destabilized the new American territory. Like employees at Sutter's Mill and Brannan's paper, soldiers deserted their posts, while inflation caused financial distress in the region. Worse, Polk knew that nations from around the world, especially the Pacific Rim, would send miners to claim the riches of California. If the U.S. did not mount a concerted effort to secure the surface riches of the land, the promise of California, which had proved contentious and controversial, would be lost. Thus, the Gold Rush was not just the extraction of a resource, but the creation of a society, ruled by American institutions, that could promote and protect the promise of California, a state poised to represent the most extreme version of the American Dream.[11]

The announcement of the discovery of gold in California and the subsequent gold rush had immediate effects on Americans and the country as a whole, as the California Geological Survey noted, "There were other important consequences, if not always fortunate ones, as a result of the gold rush. It opened the era of modern mining; it hastened the colonization of the West and the suppression and partial elimination of the Indian; it accelerated the expansion of the agricultural frontier by the need for a food supply in the gold area; and it expedited the linking of East and West."[12]

---

[10] American Presidency Project, "James K. Polk, Fourth Annual Message (Dec. 5, 1848), http://www.presidency.ucsb.edu/ws/?pid=29489
[11] American Presidency Project, "James K. Polk, Fourth Annual Message (Dec. 5, 1848), http://www.presidency.ucsb.edu/ws/?pid=29489
[12] The Discovery of Gold in California (California Geological Survey - Gold Discovery)

Chapter 3: The Argonauts

The news of California gold changed communities in the east by the very power of information. People who had initially greeted the news lukewarmly had changed their opinions drastically by the end of 1848, and many of them would now have to decide whether to leave their homes in an effort to find gold, knowing that they would be throwing caution to the wind. The very idea of the journey gave many great pause, as they knew what a trip to California would mean. Jobs and homes would not only be given up, but families as well. It was not just a decision that affected the well-to-do with connections but also the young people who had previously considered settling down in their local communities but now saw the chance to finally leave and take advantage of the tantalizing wealth in the land of California that was ostensibly available to anyone who could find gold.

This seemed to make the decision much easier, yet the men and women who left created novel solutions to solve the problem, and formed companies that, at first, were recreations of their communities. As Malcolm Rohrbough explained, "Those who determined to go often did so in a 'company' with their friends and neighbors. The company was, in truth, often a replica of the local community from which they came...The company formed and the officers chosen...Men who had been tied to labor on farms and shops suddenly found themselves officer in companies preparing to depart for California. On ethem gell such solemn duties as victualling, gathering uniforms and arms, and drafting a constitution. The hum and buzz of activity transformed their communities, and they became the envy of all those who had wished to go but decided to remain."[13]

While many left for California for personal gain, others clothed their journey in tones of patriotism and religious duties, thinking they were accomplishing the task for the goal of extending American power, society, and even the English language and the true Christian religion -- Protestantism. The fanfare that saw them off expressed itself in terms of a mighty crusade that would sweep away the former Mexican masters (and the implied laziness these Americans associated with Mexicans), as well as removing the Catholic faith brought to the land by the Spanish. In that respect, gold fever acted as a part of Manifest Destiny, and the wharves that saw the ships off to the West were carrying people who convinced themselves they were not leaving simply for their families and personal gain but for a higher cause. They would venture forth to continue the American Dream; and riches in California would be the engine of that desire.

These sentiments were on display in one of the most famous primary accounts written by a miner, one written by a man with the last name Shufelt. His letters back home have been archived by the Library of Congress, but the results of his venture to California remain unknown, as does his first name. Shufelt wrote home, "I have left those that I love as my own life behind and risked everything and endured many hardships to get here. I want to make enough to live easier and do some good with, before I return."

Though they are known as Forty-Niners today, at first the people who headed for California were known as the Argonauts, a reference to the old Greek myth about Jason and the Argonauts, and the fact that most people sailed to California instead of attempting to go over land. For those who did trek across the continent, their travels not only took them to a land few Americans had ever seen but across lands Americans knew little about, yet had heard of. For the ones who chose to go by ship, either around South America and Cape Horn, their stops took them to the Deep South, and Argonauts also came into contact with the reliquaries of the old Spanish Empire, Cuba, Argentina, Colombia, and Peru. They saw the gothic cathedrals and marveled at the near-antiquity of the "other" Americas.

Those who didn't want to sail further south to the tip of South America could choose to cross the Panamanian isthmus in the "Nueva Granada," later to be called Colombia. However, many who attempted that had their trip shortened when they came into contact with swamps full of

---

[13] Rohrbough, "'No Boys Play:' Migration and Settlement in Early Gold Rush California," *Rooted in Barbarous Soil: People, Culture, and Community in Gold Rush California*, 29.

malaria and a population that recoiled at the cultural insensitivity of the "raza yanqui." At the same time, the contact of Argonauts with Latin America would be important for later events in the coming decades.

Shufelt was one of the ones who sailed around South America, and he wrote home:

> "(We) proceeded up the river in canoes rowed by the natives, and enjoyed the scenery & howling of the monkeys & chattering of Parrots very much. We pitched our tents at Gorgona & most of our party stayed there several weeks. S. Miller & myself went on to Panama to look out for a chance to get up to San Francisco. Of our ill success you have probably been informed & consequently of our long stay there, & of the deaths in our party. Yes, here Mr. Crooker, J. Miller & L. Alden yielded up their breath to God who gave it.
>
> After many delays & vexations, we at length took passage on a German ship & set sail again on our journey to the Eldorado of the west. We went south nearly to the Equator, then turned west, the weather was warm, the winds light & contrary for our course. Our ship was a slow sailer & consequently our passage was long & tedious. One of the sailors fell from the rigging into the water & it was known that he could not swim, so the excitement was great. Ropes, planks and every thing that could be got hold of was thrown to him. He caught a plank & got on it, a boat was lowered & soon they had him on board again. He was much frightened, but not much hurt. We had one heavy squall of wind & rain, that tore the sails & broke some of the yards in pieces, & gave us a quick step motion to keep upon our feet, but soon all was right again & we were ploughing through the gentle Pacific at the rate of ten knots per hour.
>
> On the 85th day out we hove in sight of an object that greatly attracted our attention & ere long the green hills of San Francisco bay began to show their highest points, & soon we were gliding smoothly along between them, down the bay, & when the order came to let go anchor, we brought up directly in front of the City amidst a fleet of vessels, of all kinds & sizes."

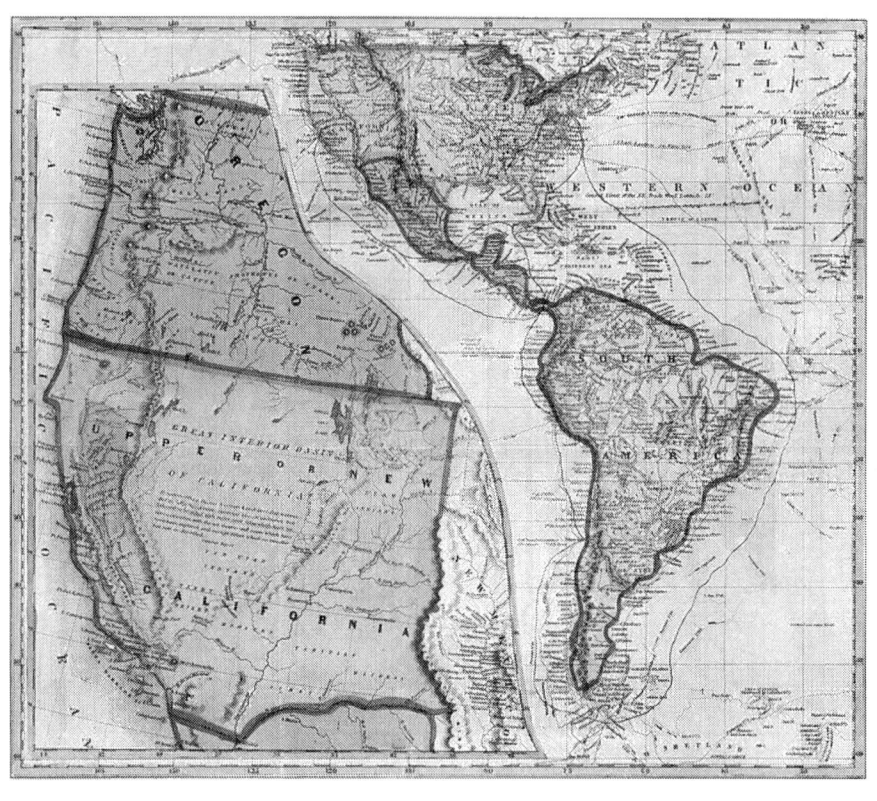
Map of water routes from the east coast to California and the Mother Lode

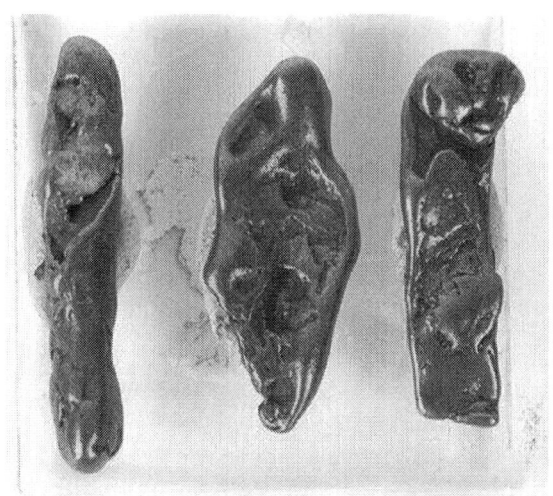

Gold nuggets found in the Mother Lode, Tuolumne County

Overland travelers faced a more dramatic journey, as the trip across the continent required a departure date in mid-May to reach the foothills of the Sierra Nevada mountains by the beginning of October, which was necessary to beat the first winter snows. This would be the first time large groups of Americans saw "the fabled symbols of the American West: the huge herds of buffalo, the dangerous Plains Indians tribes (feared but rarely seen), the towering peaks of the Rockies and the Sierra Nevada, the national monuments of Chimney Rock, Fort Laramie, and the Mormon enclave around the Great Salt Lake."[14]

All travelers, whether they arrived by sea or land, disembarked at three urban centers: San Francisco, Stockton, and Sacramento. Most miners decided to stick together, typically in groups of seven to eight people, and this personal arrangement would be all most miners ever knew. They bought their equipment together, they lived together, and they took care of each other in the camps and in the field. As Rohrbough wrote, their existence was one of intense hardship and intimacy.

> "The basic unit of work in the California Gold Rush -- at least for the first half-dozen years -- was the human body. The hard, repetitive labor of digging, carrying, and washing was often done in swift, ice-cold, moving water...Contrasting with the icy water of the snowmelt of the watercourses was the heat of the California summer, beating down on the bars and into the still

---

[14] Rohrbough, "'No Boys Play:' Migration and Settlement in Early Gold Rush California," *Rooted in Barbarous Soil: People, Culture, and Community in Gold Rush California*, 36.

canyons. The work was exhausting...So during the long work days that stretched into a long mining season, gold seekers drove themselves forward on a daily basis through a combination of restless energy, hope, self-interest, group loyalty, and sometimes desperation."[15]

Shufelt described his initial attempts to find gold:

"We hired an ox team to carry our baggage & started for this place then called Hangtown, from the fact that three persons had been hung here for stealing & attempting to murder. Ten miles from the river we passed Sutters fort, an old looking heap of buildings surrounded by an high wall of unburnt brick, & situated in the midst of a pleasant fertile plain, covered with grass and a few scattering oaks, with numerous tame cattle & mules. We walked by the wagon & at night cooked our suppers, rolled our blankets around us & lay down to rest on the ground, with nothing but the broad canopy of the heavens over us & slept soundly without fear or molestation. After leaving the plains we passed over some hills that looked dry & barren being burnt up by the sun & the long droughts that we have here. We reached this place at night on the fourth day, & in the morning found ourselves in the midst of the diggings, being surrounded by holes dug.

We pitched our tents, shouldered our picks & shovels & with pan in hand sallied forth to try our fortunes at gold digging. We did not have very good success being green at mining, but by practice & observation we soon improved some, & found a little of the shining metal. "

It is found along the banks of the streams & in the beds of the same, & in almost every little ravine putting into the streams. And often from 10 to 50 ft. from the beds up the bank. We sometimes have to dig several feet deep before we find any, in other places all the dirt & clay will pay to wash, but generally the clay pays best. If there is no clay, then it is found down on the rock. All the lumps are found on the rock--& most of the fine gold. We tell when it will pay by trying the dirt with a pan. This is called prospecting here. If it will pay from six to 12 1/2 pr pan full, then we go to work. Some wash with cradles some with what is called a tom & various other fixings. But I like the tom best of any thing that I have seen.

It is a box or trough about 8 or 9 feet long, some 18 in. wide & from 5 to 6 in. high, with an iron sieve in one end punched with 1/2 in. holes. Underneath this is placed a ripple or box with two ripples across it. The tom is then placed in an oblique position, the water is brought on by means of a hose. The dirt, stone, clay & all is then thrown in & stirred with a shovel until the water runs clear, the gold &

---

[15] Rohrbough, "'No Boys Play:' Migration and Settlement in Early Gold Rush California," *Rooted in Barbarous Soil: People, Culture, and Community in Gold Rush California*, 40-41.

finer gravel goes through the sieve & falls in the under box & lodges above the ripples. Three men can wash all day without taking this out as the water washes the loose gravel over and all the gold settles to the bottom. One man will wash as fast as two can pick & shovel it in, or as fast as three rockers or cradles."

Just as important were the living situations many found themselves in. The groups of miners shared every household task and had to cover the previously unknown sphere of domesticity that had usually been reserved to women back home. As a result miners who prided themselves on their masculine imperviousness to physical pain also had to double as cooks, seamstresses, and nurses for each other. Far from entering a recognizable world, they entered one defined by new methods of living and brand new cultures as well. Whites were hardly the only ones participating in the rush.

Shufelt, who lived in a small cabin with half a dozen other miners, explained the living conditions in a letter:

> "Many, very many, that come here meet with bad success & thousands will leave their bones here. Others will lose their health, contract diseases that they will carry to their graves with them. Some will have to beg their way home, & probably one half that come here will never make enough to carry them back. But this does not alter the fact about the gold being plenty here, but shows what a poor frail being man is, how liable to disappointments, disease & death.
>
> There is a good deal of sin & wickedness going on here, Stealing, lying, Swearing, Drinking, Gambling & murdering. There is a great deal of gambling carried on here. Almost every public House is a place for Gambling, & this appears to be the greatest evil that prevails here. Men make & lose thousands in a night, & frequently small boys will go up & bet $5 or 10 (Equivalent to $115-$225 today) -- & if they lose all, go the next day & dig more. We are trying to get laws here to regulate things but it will be very difficult to get them executed."

Chapter 4: Las Californias

Though it's often forgotten now, at the time gold was discovered in California, whites were a minority in the extreme, outnumbered by Native Americans at a rate of about 35:1 alone. That didn't even account for the Mexicans in the area. As a result, white miners came to a California formed by regions closest to it, and in no way resembling the American culture found further east on the same continent.

California did not belong to the Atlantic world that most miners had come from; the Pacific Ocean provided different flavors from Asia, Australia, the Pacific Northwest, and South America, and the camps the miners created only added to the present mix. This soon became apparent in the choice of foods they ate, from Mexican to Chilean to Chinese. Their choice of pleasurable tastes also involved the diverse selection of people from different cultures, as miners grew enamored of the different women and men in the camps, expressing desires to have sexual relations with Chileans, Mexicans, Native Americans, and with the other men too. In addition to a general lack of women in the area, many of the miners were willing to stretch gender roles and activities by engaging in relationships that subverted the usual divisions between relationships defined by male/female and man/woman. Simply put, more men than women occupied the camps, and the geographic patterns of settlement based on migration trails also made white men a minority, at least initially. As Susan Lee Johnson wrote, "This was especially true of men who lived and worked in the Southern Mines, that region in the Sierra Nevada foothills tributary to the San Joaquin River...the Southern Mines, by far the most demographically diverse of California's mining areas. At the end of the 1850s, for example, immigrants from outside the United State -- along with some African Americans and non-California Indians, such as Cherokee -- outnumbered Anglo Americans there."[16]

Geography explained the first wave of miners to immigrate to California. It was not the east coast and its Americans who came first but people from Peru, Chile, and Mexicans who arrived by ship and land. Settlers from Oregon and British Columbia -- Oregon Country -- and further abroad from Australia and New Zealand soon arrived as well. Furthermore, Hawaiians from the islands entered the minefields too. Yet even these groups were preceded by the Native Californians and the "Californio" Mexican colonists. Far from finding a place unformed, Americans merely added to the culture of the place; and the camps and their locations in California explained the differences of the world of early California. Sucheng Chan noted:

> "A significant number of British Columbians, many of whom were British-born, and Oregonians dug for the precious metal in the Trinity-Klamath-Shasta Region, which they had traversed as they journeyed southward. American Forty-Niners who had cross the Great Plains and the Rocky Mountains dominate the Northern Mines in Plumas, Butte, Sierra, Yuba, Nevada, Placer, El Dorado, and Amador counties because southern branch of the California Trail cut through the Sierra Nevada at the Carson Pass and Donner Pass, which led to the Northern Mines. The largest contingent of Latin Americans prospected in the Southern Mines -- in Calaveras, Tuolumne, and Mariposa counties -- because as they trekked northward they reached that area first."[17]

---

[16] Johnson, *Rooted in Barbarous Soil: People, Culture, and Community in Gold Rush California*, "'My Own Private Life': Toward a History of Desire in Gold Rush California," 316.

[17] Chan, *Rooted in Barbarous Soil: People, Culture, and Community in Gold Rush California*," A People of Exceptional Character": Ethnic Diversity, Nativism, and Racism in the California Gold Rush," 54-55.

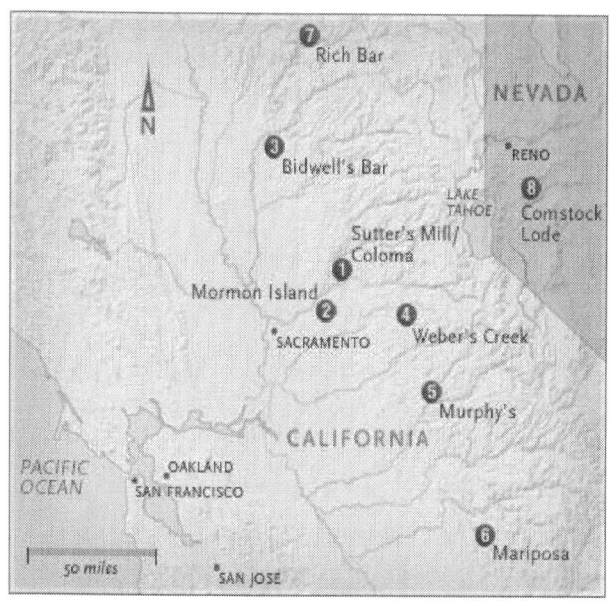

Early miner camps

The Californios belonged to the first generation of Mexican colonists to be born in *Las Californias*, with dreams of a more democratic state and a stronger, less-mercantalist economy. The coming of the Americans and the Gold Rush were initially things that the Mexican colonists wanted to turn to their advantage. They had learned to recognize the U.S.'s previous rehearsals for invasion, but the feeling grew among the Mexican elites on the Californian frontier that the future prosperity of Alta California lay with negotiated relationships with the American settlers. Such a plan would remove the biggest threats to Californio aspirations: the Church and the military. The Franciscans had successfully laid claim to Alta California following the Sacred Expedition of 1769-1770, but the establishment of the religious order's 21 missions and the presidio-based colonial military proved a challenge until the liberal reforms of the Mexican nation following the collapse of Emperor Agustin Iturbide "empire" in 1830s Mexico. With that, the Californios finally broke the power of the Franciscan order and took advantage of the secularization program that targeted the missions of Alta California.

The Californios longed for a Mexico that granted them entrepreneurial freedom, which had languished during Spain's calculated isolation of the Californias, treating the territory as a mere frontier buffer zone against Native American and American invasions. But after the removal of the Franciscan power in the missions, the Californios not only expanded their already-large estates but were able to intercede in the lives of Natives who the mission priests had claimed dominion over. Though the Californios professed a liberal treatment of the natives, the intimate relationship they fostered with the natives turned oppressive in its paternalism. The Native Americans provided a function to the ranching economy of the Californio baronial estates, working in most cases for the bare pay of subsistence, while their overlords looked lazily after their education and forced them to adopt Christianity and a European lifestyle. The Californio lords would take advantage of this labor arrangement during the initial stage of the Gold Rush, when the ranch owners traded the natives food for their labor in the gold fields.[18]

The Californios stood to gain the most from the Gold Rush because of their long-standing attempts to remain autonomous from the central government of Mexico. They not only battled with government officers; families in the northern and southern Alta California battled one another for control of the provincial government. In 1844, two years before the Mexican-American War, the two sections of the state united against the Mexican governor, Michetorena, and two years later at the Battle of La Providencia, defeated the governor, who then left Alta California. Mexico no longer controlled Alta California, which would operate like an independent nation until the end of the American-led Bear Flag Rebellion, when the U.S. Army finally seized control of the state. By 1848, Alta California's enjoyed a state of de facto independence, though the region lay divided by rival regimes in the north and south.[19]

The Californios in the south ultimately ended up doing better than their northern compatriots due to the impact of the Gold Rush on the San Francisco Bay Area. For a period of time, the cattle of the southern ranches became sought after, in order to feed the miners. The Californios successfully led cattle drives up the coast and San Joaquin Valley to the buyer's market of their beef. For a period of years in the early Gold Rush, the Californios near the Mission of San Diego enjoyed the greatest financial success. However, the exchange rate of gold and spending habits drastically reordered their world and caused an eventual decline. For one, the greater deal has been placed on the sudden wealth the Californios had because of the Gold Rush. They spent exorbitantly, as some historians claim; and this might be true, but the arrival of thousands of new Californians made products scarce, driving up costs for goods that everyone struggled to pay, Californios included.[20]

In retrospect, the most significant development that changed the financial fortunes of the Californios involved the re-alignment of the commercial center of California from the south to the north in San Francisco. Suddenly marginalized, and bested by later competitors, the Californios of the south could not engage in any profitable trade due to high freight costs. This ultimately impoverished them and left them financially vulnerable to the long period of litigation

---

[18] Rose Marie Beebe and Robert M. Senkewicz, *Chonicles of Early California, 1535-1846: Lands of Promise and Despair*, 341, 345, 375, 390; Californios, "Californios, A People and a Culture," http://www.californios.us/ca/
[19] The California State Military Museum, "Spanish and Mexican California: Battle of La Providencia (Second Battle of Cahuenga Pass), http://www.militarymuseum.org/LaProvidencia.html
[20] The Journal of San Diego History, "The Decline of the Californios: The Case of San Diego (1846-1856)," http://www.sandiegohistory.org/journal/75summer/decline.htm

that followed American conquest. The loss of land from the Board of Land Commissioners made it nearly impossible for them to turn their full attention to the opportunities of the Gold Rush. Years spent in court defending their land claims finally bankrupted most of the ranchers, who were forced to sell their property to pay legal costs.[21]

The large number of merchant vessels in San Francisco's harbor is quickly apparent in this picture, taken circa 1850-1851

---

[21] The Journal of San Diego History, "The Decline of the Californios: The Case of San Diego (1846-1856)," http://www.sandiegohistory.org/journal/75summer/decline.htm

Chapter 5: Dealing with Demographics

Roy D. Graves' illustration of Chinese miners

The flow of Chinese immigrants increased dramatically in 1852, sparked in large part by a crop failure in southern China that caused the custom houses in San Francisco to swell with 20,026 Chinese arrivals. Even more Chinese came as news reached China about the apparent ease of mining in California. By the end of the decade, ⅛ of the population of the Southern Mines consisted of Chinese miners. Chinese miners would become known as the most industrious and tireless of the miners, finding gold in claims that previous owners had thought depleted and persisting in mining an area far longer than others who eventually left the fields altogether.

However, other miners reacted to their presence negatively, and in some cases Chinese miners had their camps violently attacked. The state government attempted to rectify the problem through the creation of a second Miner's Tax, but unfortunately this only seemed to accelerate other miners' attacks on Chinese camps. Reports in the same year indicated that an epidemic of robberies hit the immigrant miners from China, close to 200 alone, along with a series of murders.

All of this can partly explain why the Chinese decided to diversify and choose occupations that did not put them into open competition with white American miners. Another reason, and one closer to the financial windfalls that occurred during the Gold Rush, is explained by the chance for profit in the mercantile and service industries. The Chinese moved into the laundry business, other domestic services, and later railroad building, all of which necessarily thrived as the population in the region boomed. Taking some of these businesses was also acts of gender subversion, at least by the standards of European Americans -- men just did not undertake careers usually thought of as domestic chores. For the Chinese, necessity and less aversion to these jobs brought profits, but these jobs also created more feelings of alienation between the Argonauts and the foreign-born miners.[22]

The Chinese could never overcome the legal obstacles towards true success and acceptance in Californian society during the Gold Rush, and the discriminatory procedures that prevented Chinese immigrants from full protection under the law would have had little power if not for the state apparatus that legitimized and enforced racism, namely the California Supreme Court.[23] As one historian explained, "In the case *People v. Hall*, the California Supreme Court reversed the conviction of George Hall and two other white men who had murdered a Chinese man. Hall and his companions had been convicted based on testimony of some Chinese witnesses. In its reversal the court extended the California law that African Americans and Native Americans could not testify in court to include the Chinese. The reversal made it impossible to prosecute violence against Chinese immigrants."[24]

Demographically, the numbers of blacks and Chinese also contributed to the diversity of the gold fields and the culture of the earliest days of California, which became a state in 1850. Black people had come from Latin America, but the largest number of them had come from the U.S., and 5,000 African-Americans lived in California by 1852. The largest numbers came as slaves of Southern masters who intended to personally use them in the gold fields or rent them out as laborers for other men, but some free blacks were drawn by the allure of gold themselves.

The presence of African-Americans also had a major influence on what kind of society California would be. The presence of blacks lay at the heart of the constitutional convention of the state of California, because slavery was a highly contentious issue at the time. With so much new territory to carve into states, the balance of Congressional power became a hot topic for the nation, and it had been since the people of Missouri sought to be admitted to the Union in 1819 with slavery being legal in the new state. While Congress was dealing with that, Alabama was admitted in December 1819, creating an equal number of free states and slave states. Thus, allowing Missouri to enter the Union as a slave state would disrupt the balance.

---

[22] The Gold Rush, "People and Events: Chinese Immigrants and the Gold Rush," http://www.pbs.org/wgbh/amex/goldrush/peopleevents/p_chinese.html
[23] The Gold Rush, "People and Events: Chinese Immigrants and the Gold Rush," http://www.pbs.org/wgbh/amex/goldrush/peopleevents/p_chinese.html
[24] Chinese Immigrants and the Gold Rush

Congress ultimately got around this issue by establishing what became known as the Missouri Compromise. Legislation was passed that admitted Maine as a free state, thus balancing the number once Missouri joined as a slave state. Moreover, slavery would be excluded from the Missouri Territory north of the parallel 36°30′ north, which was the southern border of Missouri itself. As a slave state, Missouri would obviously serve as the lone exception to that line.

The Missouri Compromise of 1820 staved off the crisis for the time being, but by setting a line that excluded slave states above the parallel, it would also become incredibly contentious. After the Mexican-American War ended in 1848, the sectional crisis was brewing like never before, with California and the newly-acquired Mexican territory now ready to be organized into states. The country was once again left trying to figure out how to do it without offsetting the slave-free state balance. With the new territory acquired in the Mexican-American War, pro and anti-slavery groups were at an impasse. The Whig Party supported the Wilmot Proviso, which would have banned slavery in all territory acquired from Mexico, but the slave states would have none of it. Even after Texas was annexed as a slave state, the enormous new territory would doubtless contain many other new states, and the North hoped to limit slavery as much as possible in the new territories.

Delegates to the California conventions expressed concerns about the presence of slaves in the language of other anti-slavery people, who saw the institution as a threat to free labor and the power of large businesses. But at the same time, there were so many advocates for slavery in the convention, mostly from southern California, that at one point there was a serious conversation about splitting up California into two states, one free and one slave. That said, the real weight of the conversation, which explained the crisis at the convention, revolved around whether or not any blacks should be allowed to enter the state at all.

California effectively created exceptions to the legal system in order to control the numbers of blacks and Chinese. While the state did not bar African-Americans from entering, it did prevent them from taking legal action to protect themselves from discrimination. Blacks mined, but they could never really live the lives they wanted to in a "free California." Discrimination was much more severe against the Chinese, as the Miners Tax meant their profits as laborers were severely curtailed. As for the matter of allowing the Chinese to enter the state, exclusion would come much later during the final stages of the Gold Rush, when, once again, class issues and ideas about the corruption of big business would come into play. Nevertheless, Chinese did face "commutative tolls" for entering the state. For the Chinese and African Americans, social stratification hardened, and race truly determined how certain groups labored, where they lived, and what rights they had in the courts. Chan explains:

> "This process of stratification had begun during the Spanish and Mexican periods, but it accelerate with the Gold Rush. The creation of such a hierarchy involved five sub-processes vis-a-vis peoples of color: the *exploitation* of their labor, the *denial* of their civil rights, the *aversion* of social contracts with them,

the *deprivation* of their chances for upward mobility, and the insistence on *deference* in the behavior toward the European American majority. The rapid emergence of such an unequal society -- one that goes against the professed American creed -- is one of the darker legacies of the Gold Rush."[25]

Of course, there was also the matter of Native Americans, of which there were upwards of about 150,000 in California. The Native Americans of California faced intense hatred from the Forty-Niners, initially due to their labor relationship with the Californio barons. Some of the first white Americans to mine gold came from Oregon Country; and as they moved south into the Klamath Mountains of Northern California, they encountered the first Californio ranches, where landowners used natives as laborers for the mining of gold. The sight of Indian workers, working mostly for subsistence and not pay, enraged the Oregonians because the institution of work the Californios used had the appearance of slavery.

The removal of Native Americans from California was harshest in the north; over the course of about 12 years, the population went from 150,000 Native Americans in 1848 to 35,000 in 1860. This coincided with the destruction of the economic power of the Californios, who relied upon the native workforce to mine gold, as well as the new tactic of the federal government to relocate natives to reservations. At first, the state passed laws that allowed miners to conscript natives as indentured servants. Then the young government encouraged private militias and individual citizens to play a role in the removal of Native Americans in California.

The removal of Native Americans had several benefits for the Forty-Niners. It opened up more mining areas to them and removed a lot of competition. Not surprisingly, the same policy of removal happened near the Southern Mines in central and southern California, as white settlers wanted the 7.5 percent of California's land area that treaties had set aside for Native Americans. Squatters also moved onto reservation lands in the hopes of securing parcels that gave them access to the foothills of the Sierras, where the mining took place. Except for the surrender of Modoc resisters, who moved onto reservations after defeat at the hands of the U.S. Army, the Native Americans were forcibly removed until most tribes existed as only a few bands.

Perhaps not surprisingly, the groups that prospered in the initial stage of the Gold Rush were the ones that were geographically closer than any group, mainly Mexicans from the state of Sonora, the Californios from Alta California, and the Mormon pioneers from "Deseret" (later to be known as the territory of Utah). These groups stood in the best position to prosper from the mining of gold. Their experience with the terrain and the type of mining put them in the best position, but they also proved invaluable to the other miners for the level of expertise and techniques they would bring to the mining of gold in California. The Sonorans' style of mining was not the method most people associate with the Gold Rush, placer (surface) mining in rivers

---

[25] Chan, *Rooted in Barbarous Soil: People, Culture, and Community in Gold Rush California*," A People of Exceptional Character": Ethnic Diversity, Nativism, and Racism in the California Gold Rush," 79.

using pans. Instead, the Sonorans used "dry mining." The California Geological Survey explains, "As a method of mining it was simple, crude and inefficient, but it had the advantage of being inexpensive. After the pay dirt was dug, it was sun dried on a large canvas and then pulverized into dust. The next operation was to throw the dirt by the panful into the air in order to allow the wind to blow away the lighter elements and to let the gold dust fall back into the pan. Thus the old agricultural procedure of winnowing was the first method used extensively in California mining; for not only was it used in the Los Angeles area, but also it was introduced by many of these same Sonorans into the mines of the Sierra Nevada after 1848."[26]

The creation of the state of California during the Gold Rush meant the young state was forced to contend with the Californios, who owned a lot of land but engaged in a form of economy that left them nearly destitute in a region that now swelled with the wealth of the riches dug out of the earth. The Gold Rush gave the ranch barons in the south a significant boost, but they eventually became impoverished, and most lost their lands as the economy transformed into one where whites became increasingly involved in the mercantile business. As men like Samuel Brannan determined, commerce was the real "gold" to be found in California during the Gold Rush.[27]

---

[26] The Discovery of Gold in California (California Geological Survey - Gold Discovery)
[27] Sandos, "'Because he is a liar and a thief': Conquering the Residents of 'Old' California, 1850-1880," *Rooted in Barbarous Soil: People, Culture and Community in Gold Rush California.*

Chapter 6: Golden Dreams Without Golden Rules

Illustration depicting whites, Native Americans, and blacks mining gold together

If harmony existed in the California gold fields of 1848, the arrival of the Forty-Niners, the first large wave of Argonauts, changed all that. They noticed the supremacy of knowledge by the Spanish-speaking miners, especially the successful techniques of the Mexicans from the state of Sonora, who had mined in Mexico and in southern California and could extract large quantities of gold in low-running streams or dry hillsides. American arrivals framed their outrage with these miners in terms of class antagonism, for many believed that the Spanish Californios were elites who benefitted from the labor of natives or the Sonorans, who they described as peasants working on the behest of Mexican mine owners back in Mexico. To American Argonauts, many of whom belonged to the Democratic Party, this appeared to violate egalitarian principles that they intended to bring to California. These social goals were expressed by attempts at creating rules for mining that practiced American social mores and ethics based on free enterprise and democracy. Chan explained how a system of land claims was quickly set up, "Each individual could hold only one claim, except for the person who made the find, who was entitled to two claim. The claim had to be officially recorded an elected recorder. To hold a claim, a miner had to work it a specified number of days per specified time period. Thus, miner enjoyed only usufructuary rights over their claim, with disputes settled at miners' meeting or the recorder of alcalde [mayor]."[28]

Ultimately, the strongest current of hatred involved feelings of racism cloaked in U.S. nationalism. The Forty-Niners felt that since the U.S. had conquered the territory from Mexico, citizens of the nation that controlled California owned full rights to the land, not immigrants from other nations. On top of that, many of the miners had been supporters of the Mexican-American War or even veterans of the fighting, which made them feel even more entitled to California and its gold. There's also no doubt many saw the presence of Catholic, Spanish-speaking, brown skinned people as anathema to the creation of a free, democratic, and industrious California.

The Forty-Niners responded with violence, and then laws, to try to keep foreign miners out of the gold fields. It was not uncommon for white miners to attack non-whites, especially when the 1850 Foreign Miners' Tax gave them the impression that more acts of violence were permitted by law. Eventually, the pressures of Argonauts appeared to pay off, as more Latino miners were expelled from the southern mines, and an exodus resulted later on. However, this attempt proved partially short-lived, as merchants from the region began to lose money without the presence of miners and their gold.

This led to a repeal of the tax, but that did not bring an end to the discrimination. Race played an even larger role in the attempts by Forty-Niners to expel Chinese immigrants and African-Americans from the fields. This was largely because the nature of mining had changed from surface mining to more capital-intensive systems of extracting the gold, such as river, deep shaft or quartz, and hydraulic mining; and cheap labor was needed by the mining corporations.

The use of taxes and violence was facilitated by the fact that California was so far away from the rest of the nation, because establishing a society based on the search and extraction of mineral wealth in a wilderness area created profound problems for San Francisco and California that had far-reaching social consequences. The founders of the city and state were, in every sense of the word, on a quest for riches, and they wanted to promote and sustain this enterprise by a careful mix of regulation and laissez faire. In addition to racial tensions, there was also a tension between government and businesses that invested in the development of the state.

In this kind of environment, San Francisco and the gold fields naturally became a place fraught with cultural diversity and a propensity for violence and lawlessness. The wildness of California does not suggest that the new society did not possess cultural expressions of civil life, as San Francisco did serve as cultural hub of transmission of different clubs, cooperatives, and associations for the promotion of civic life, such as the arts and education, and San Francisco had municipal organizations that would, at least in theory, improve society. However, San Francisco,

---

[28] Chan, *Rooted in Barbarous Soil: People, Culture, and Community in Gold Rush California*," A People of Exceptional Character": Ethnic Diversity, Nativism, and Racism in the California Gold Rush," 59.
28

as an urban center, demonstrated the types of extremes that one would expect of a society based off the dream of instant financial dreams. For the majority that suffered a bust instead of a boom, the failures and disappointments resulted in political upheaval, economic uncertainty, and cycles of violence.[29]

By any measure, these were the conditions of vigilantism in a state with a full constitution that possessed the institutions of a republic but denied civil rights to Californios, Native Americans, Latinos, Hawaiians, and Asians. In a climate where civil rights were easily sidestepped, the rise of violence became its own form of civil development, because the violence was not always random and irrational. There would prove to be a great deal of organization and thought behind the use of force to make sure everyone obeyed the legal rights set forth by the state's constitution.[30]

In his seminal study of American westward expansion and the process of state-making, the notion of the frontier, as explained by Frederick Jackson Turner in 1890, was one of American self-rule and enterprise. This helps explains how California was afflicted in its efforts to self-organize during the Gold Rush, as pointed out by Mary Floyd Williams:

> "It was the multiplicity of revolutionary associations, and the ease with which they might run into the form taken by the Vigilance Committees of the far West, that led even so ardent a follower of revolutionary principles as Patrick Henry to declare in 1786 regarding the defenseless condition of the western frontier, "that protection which is the best and general object of social compact is withdrawn, and the people, thus consigned to destruction, will naturally form associations, disgraceful as they are destructive of government."[31]

While the "Wild West" has long been romanticized, a more accurate portrayal of the American frontier is one about the way men and women joined extralegal organizations to support and enforce the law in the federal territories and new states. In many cases, citizens defined themselves as "regulators," considering themselves a contingency in the event that the legal systems in a state suffered from corruption. Naturally, these extralegal organizations weren't afraid to use violence, justifying their actions by claiming the lack of authorities in the area left it up to them. Put simply, the regulators were vigilantes.[32]

In the case of San Francisco and California during the Gold Rush, instances of political corruption did give rise to vigilantism, but the presence of so-called "law and order" groups, ironically, provoked an extralegal response from San Francisco's business leaders, who feared

---

[29] Ohlone College, "Gold Rush and California Statehood," http://www.ohlone.edu/instr/english/elc/engl163/goldrush.html
[30] Gold Fever, "Law, Order, and Justice for Some," http://museumca.org/goldrush/fever16.html;
[31] Mary Floyd Williams, *History of the San Francisco Committee of the Vigilance of 1851*, 13-14, quoted from Turner, F.J, "Western State-Making," *American Historical Review*, I (1895-1896), 265-266.
[32] Mary Floyd Williams, *History of the San Francisco Committee of the Vigilance of 1851*

that vigilante groups threatened the democratic and economic health of the state. Violence took the form of racist attacks on foreigners and non-whites who worked in the gold fields, and in these cases, "law and order" groups were seen as wanton, uncontrollable groups by the elites, despite the claim by Forty-Niners that immigrant miners did not obey the laws that governed gold mining claims. Whether or not this was true, the perception of vigilantism's threat to democracy could not be ignored. When gangs of unemployed miners attacked non-white miners, business leaders realized it threatened the civic order that businessmen needed to thrive. Order had to inhabit a region that produced favorable outcomes for the creation and sustainability of wealth.[33]

The Vigilance Committees of 1851 and 1856 should not viewed as the actions of men on the margins of society, but as the organization of men from the business community of San Francisco who had little faith in the men who occupied political office in the city. They had even less faith in the "law and order" forces that regulated the mining camps in the countryside.[34] The Vigilance Committee announced:

> "WHEREAS it has become apparent to the citizens of San Francisco, that there is no security for life and property, either under the regulations of society as it at present exists, or under the law as now administered; *Therefore* the citizens, whose names are hereunto attached, do unit themselves into an association for the maintenance of the peace and good order of society, and the preservation of the lives and property of the citizens of San Francisco, and do bind ourselves, each unto the other, to do and perform every lawful act for the maintenance of law and order, and to sustain the laws when faithfully and properly administered; but we are determined that no thief, burglar, incendiary or assassin, shall escape punishment, either by the quibbles of the law, the insecurity of prisons. the carelessness or corruption of the police, or a laxity of those who pretend to administer justice."[35]

---

[33] *The Examiner*, "San Francisco Law and Order Forces Defeated," http://www.examiner.com/article/san-francisco-law-and-order-forces-defeated; "Vigilante Justice in the Gold Mines," http://www.examiner.com/article/vigilante-justice-the-mines; History Engine, "Crime and Instant Justice in Gold Rush California," http://historyengine.richmond.edu/episodes/view/5127; Calisphere, 1848-1856: Gold Rush Era, "Murder and Mayhem," http://www.calisphere.universityofcalifornia.edu/themed_collections/subtopic1a.html; SF Genealogy: San Francisco History, "The Annals of San Francisco (Part three: The Hounds), http://www.sfgenealogy.com/sf/history/hbann3-1.htm

[34] Maritime Heritage Project, "The Vigilance Committee," http://www.maritimeheritage.org/vips/vigilance.html

[35] Maritime Heritage Project, "The Vigilance Committee," http://www.maritimeheritage.org/vips/vigilance.html

Of these men, Samuel Brannan served as the most important member, and founder, of the first committee. Brannan employed citizens as private "safety committees" to round up the criminal element in San Francisco and its environs, negate the deleterious effects of politicians they deemed ineffective against corruption, and judge and execute all peoples guilty of acts that threatened the civil health of the municipality and the state. Brannan, along with his business associates, presided, either directly or indirectly, over the arrest, tribunals, and corporal punishment of residents of California. This not only took the form of public trials and executions but even the creation of private armies -- sharpshooter brigades -- who engaged in paramilitary operations against vigilante forces inside and outside the city. Gangs of criminals, like the "Sydney Ducks" and bands of anti-foreigner nativists, the Hounds, were destroyed or exiled from the city. Later, safety committees raided illegal gambling and opium dens in San Francisco to police the moral behavior of a city that had grown more worldly and uncontrollable than the city boosters were comfortable with.[36]

Despite the efforts of vigilance committees, vigilantism was part and parcel of an unregulated society born out of an impulse to get rich quick. After all, mining laws actually encouraged people to take risks and "jump the claim" that another legally owned; violence arose because claim holders and claim jumpers were equally protected under the law. This created chronic insecurity and litigation, not to mention conditions that encouraged miners to disrespect the

---

[36] *The Examiner*, "San Francisco Law and Order Forces Defeated," http://www.examiner.com/article/san-francisco-law-and-order-forces-defeated; "Vigilante Justice in the Gold Mines," http://www.examiner.com/article/vigilante-justice-the-mines; History Engine, "Crime and Instant Justice in Gold Rush California," http://historyengine.richmond.edu/episodes/view/5127; Calisphere, 1848-1856: Gold Rush Era, "Murder and Mayhem," http://www.calisphere.universityofcalifornia.edu/themed_collections/subtopic1a.html; SF Genealogy: San Francisco History, "The Annals of San Francisco (Part three: The Hounds), http://www.sfgenealogy.com/sf/history/hbann3-1.htm

claims of others. Miners thought the odds were in their favor and were rewarded at times. Given the chance to successfully steal the value of someone's land, which was limited and not always fixed until someone actually mined the property, it's no wonder that some disgruntled miners resorted to violence to right what they perceived as wrongs inflicted upon them.[37]

Chapter 7: Mining the Miners

The vigilance committees were established by the same men who had overseen a significant business revolution in mercantile products throughout California. While the Gold Rush will always conjure images of miners trying to find gold, most of the wealth was not in the hands of the miners in the fields but in the hands of the people trying to cater to the miners and sell them goods. Of course, as businesses generated more wealth in California, it produced an economic climate that jived with the risk-taking mentality of the gold rush. Entrepreneurs took bigger chances, and some produced their own type of booms. Kasler explained:

> "Some of the entrepreneurs started businesses that endured into the 20th century. Domenico Ghirardelli sold general merchandise to miners before devoting his full attention to chocolates. Korbel Champagne Cellars started as a maker of cigar boxes. John Studebaker made wheelbarrows for miners in Placerville, launching the company that eventually would make automobiles in Indiana. William Tecumseh Sherman co-owned a provisions shop in Coloma and was a banker in San Francisco before he became a legend of the Civil War. In Sacramento, the Rivett carpet company and Fuller-O'Brien paint company started out as one company, peddling glass and wall coverings. The four major titans of early California business -- Stanford, Crocker, Hopkins and Huntington -- made their money selling hardware in Sacramento before they moved to San Francisco and became railroad barons. There was tremendous land speculation; Front Street lots would change hands a dozen times a month."[38]

---

[37] Karen Clay, Gavin Wright, "Order Without Law? Property Rights During the California Gold Rush," Explorations in Economic History, http://www.stanford.edu/~write/papers/Order%20Without%20Law.pdf

[38] Gold Rush (Part Four: The Legacy), "Businesses, Banks Cashed in by 'Mining the Miners,'" http://www.calgoldrush.com/lb_sets/04business.html

Portsmouth Square in San Francisco during the Gold Rush

Meanwhile, miners attempted to sidestep the obstacles to instant wealth through their own associations and cooperatives. As the easy gold in rivers and streams "dried up," many had quickly come to realize that control over water would allow them to mine dryer terrain and climates. The companies that formed made miners employees in most cases, and some made a great deal of money. Control over water led to the innovation of hydraulic mining, which proved highly successful. Kasler writes, "As mining techniques became more sophisticated, so did these corporations. Early on, the miners used their own funds to start companies; they were the owners. By the mid-'50s there were companies with 50 to 100 miners -- many working as employees, for a day's wage -- backed by $200,000 or so in capital, much of it from New York or London."[39]

---

[39] Gold Rush (Part Four: The Legacy), "Businesses, Banks Cashed in by 'Mining the Miners,'" http://www.calgoldrush.com/lb_sets/04business.html
[39] Gold Rush (Part Four: The Legacy), "Businesses, Banks Cashed in by 'Mining the Miners,'" http://www.calgoldrush.com/lb_sets/04business.html

Miners using jets of water to excavate water from gravel beds

However, miners could not avoid the increasing connection between California's economy and the world. Finance capital did not need worker cooperatives; in fact, many businesses were better off with fewer workers, because improvements in mining technology required less miners to obtain the gold. Bigger machines extracted more of the surface earth, but the price of the mining technology grew enough to exclude more miners from the possibility of ever owning a company or even a stake in a company. Access to capital meant corporations could grow and expand the franchise of ownership to stockholders with access to capital, and of course, these stockholders could be businessmen completely removed from the region with no knowledge about how the mining actually worked.

To a large extent, San Francisco's rise to become one of the commercial centers of California occurred because of the presence of banking giants. The original service economy of the state worked on the exchange of gold dust, but this monetary system proved unstable and increasingly untenable in a world exchange economy. Banks rose up and private mints made coins, and the creation a U.S. Mint finally took place in 1854.

As it turned out, the rise of banks provoked a panic in 1855 that ruined the fortunes of miners with investments in banks. Bank runs took place and banks collapsed. One survivor of the bank failures was Wells Fargo; so many investors ended up in debt to Wells Fargo that the bank giant's biggest source of wealth came from the ownership of corporations.[40]

Over time, the rise of banks like Wells Fargo meant that corporations controlled the gold mines, and access to technology meant that the appearance of mining changed. The ability to accomplish the task of clearing away hundreds of thousands of years of sediment allowed hydraulic mining to take place; and the diversion of water, no small task even for a company, allowed dams to store water. The companies then used pumps and levers to apply extreme high pressure.[41]

Illustration of miners excavating a dry bed after the water has been diverted

---

[40] Gold Rush (Part Four: The Legacy), "Businesses, Banks Cashed in by 'Mining the Miners,'" http://www.calgoldrush.com/lb_sets/04business.html; Wells Fargo, "Since 1852," https://www.wellsfargo.com/about/history/adventure/since_1852
[41] The Discovery of Gold in California (California Geological Survey - Gold Discovery), http://www.conservation.ca.gov/cgs/geologic_resources/gold/CA_GoldDiscovery_files/Pages/GoldDiscovery.aspx

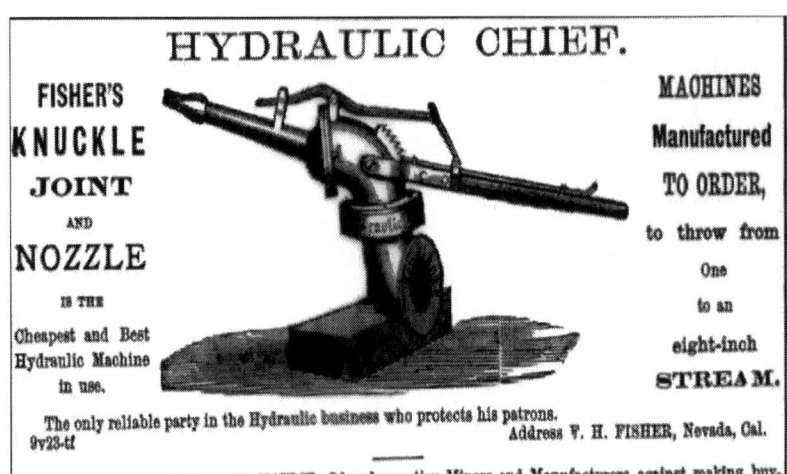

Advertisement for a hydraulic monitor

The corporations used mammoth monitors to get to the gold, some 14-16 feet long, blasting the hillsides and cratering mountains. 1.5 billion cubic yards of debris was washed down hillsides and into streams and valleys. Some river systems and wetlands were permanently buried under sand and rock. One observer commented on the damage.

> "Tornado, flood, earthquake and volcano combined could hardly make greater havoc, spread wider ruin and wreck, than are to be seen everywhere in the track of the larger gold-washing operations. None of the interior streams of California, though naturally pure as crystal, escape the change to a thick yellow mud from this cause, early in their progress from the hills. The Sacramento River is worse than the Missouri. Many of the streams are turned out of their original channels, either directly for mining purposes, or in consequence of the great masses of soil and gravel that come down from the gold-washing above. Thousands of acres of fine land along their banks are ruined forever by the deposits of this character. A farmer may have his whole estate turned into a barren waste by a flood of sand and gravel from some hydraulic mining up stream; more, if a fine orchard or garden stands in the way of the working of a rich gulch or bank, orchard or garden must go. Then the tornout, dug- out, washed to pieces and then washed over sidehills, masses that have been or are being subjected to the hydraulics of the miners, are the very devil's chaos indeed. The country is full of them among the mining

districts of the Sierra Nevada, and they are truly a terrible blot upon the face of Nature."[42]

Hydraulic mining

Though it's often forgotten, the major environmental impact of mining is what truly ended the California Gold Rush. At the peak of production, the environmental damage became so pronounced, with debris flooding and destroying farmland and preventing river traffic, that the farmers organized and demanded that legislators in Sacramento force the corporations to end the practice. In 1884, the California Supreme Court finally forced businesses to stop the destruction. This ruling ended the era of quick riches from gold mining, thus ending the boom period. More importantly, it was farming, not mining, that was king of California now.[43]

> "The economic consequences and significance of the discovery of gold are equally great but harder to determine. Increased production in the United States, followed by increased foreign production resulting from the California gold rush, caused an increase of money in circulation. By 1865 in California alone $750,000,000 in gold had been mined, and this figure is considered a conservative estimate. In spite of the heavy

---

[42] Sierra College, "Monitors - Water Cannons of Hydraulic Mining," http://www.sierracollege.edu/ejournals/jsnhb/v2n1/monitors.html
[43] Gold Fever! "Giant Gold Machines - Hydraulic Mining," http://museumca.org/goldrush/fever19-hy.html

increase of circulating gold, the much-feared serious inflation, which was predicted by economists, failed to materialize. True, in California, at the source of gold and where commodities were scarce, initial inflation was tremendous; but world inflation as a result of the California gold rush and its successors, was slight."[44]

Chapter 8: The Legacy of the Gold Rush

The California Gold Rush will always evoke images of the common man panning for gold along the rivers and foothills of California, but of the 118 million ounces of gold that have been extracted from California since the discovery of gold there, most of it was accomplished through mining rocks and hard materials, the kinds of activities that lone miners couldn't accomplish by themselves. Some of the early miners unquestionably made fortunes worth millions of dollars in today's currency, but they were the exception to the rule. The wealthiest men in California during the Gold Rush were men like Samuel Brannan, who sold shovels and pickaxes to miners rather than attempt to strike gold himself. Levi Strauss made a fortune selling denim overalls to miners, and his name is still well-known in America as a jeans manufacturer.

Illustration of miners crushing quartz ore to find and extract the gold

In the immediate wake of the discovery of gold, California formed from the forces of the Gold Rush that intended to reward free enterprise and risk-taking individualism but also prevent undesirable competitors from challenging white Americans on the frontier. But the search for

---

[44] The Discovery of Gold in California (California Geological Survey - Gold Discovery), http://www.conservation.ca.gov/cgs/geologic_resources/gold/CA_GoldDiscovery_files/Pages/GoldDiscovery.aspx

riches in California, as well as other regions that helped support boomtowns throughout the frontier, also helped to bridge the new continental empire of the U.S. In addition to spurring westward expansion, wealth was created not just by mineral riches but by the creation of a vibrant economy that functioned in step with the rest of the global market. Americans appreciated that the achievement of instant wealth was possible, but they also witnessed the rapid growth of banks and corporations that created a state to support the monopolization of natural resources. The creation of California could not have happened without the arrival of gold, but it was not gold by itself that explained the passions of the "gold rush." Americans were committed to the ambitions of a nation to dominate the continent, and the Gold Rush was a manifestation of that Manifest Destiny.

Bibliography

Bancroft, Hubert Howe (1884–1890) History of California, vols. 18–24.

Brands, H. W. (2003). The age of gold: the California Gold Rush and the new American dream. New York: Anchor Books.

Heizer, Robert F. (1974). The destruction of California Indians. Lincoln and London: University of Nebraska Press.

Hill, Mary (1999). Gold: the California story. Berkeley and Los Angeles: University of California Press.

Holliday, J. S. (1999). Rush for riches: Gold fever and the making of California. Oakland, California, Berkeley and Los Angeles: Oakland Museum of California and University of California Press.

Johnson, Susan Lee (2001). Roaring Camp: the social world of the California Gold Rush. New York: W. W. Norton & Company.

Rawls, James, J.; Bean, Walton (2003). California: An interpretive history. New York: McGraw-Hill.

Starr, Kevin (1973). Americans and the California dream: 1850–1915. New York and Oxford: Oxford University Press.

Starr, Kevin and Richard J. Orsi (eds.) (2000). Rooted in barbarous soil: people, culture, and community in Gold Rush California. Berkeley and Los Angeles: University of California Press.

Printed in Great Britain
by Amazon.co.uk, Ltd.,
Marston Gate.